THE
ANCIENT
EGYPTIANS

With special thanks to Megan Cifarelli,
Norbert Schimmel Fellow in the Art of the Mediterranean
at The Metropolitan Museum of Art, New York City,
for her invaluable assistance in
reading the manuscript.

CULTURES
OF THE PAST

THE
ANCIENT
EGYPTIANS

ELSA MARSTON

BENCHMARK BOOKS

MARSHALL CAVENDISH
NEW YORK

**For Miss Cutts, my fourth-grade teacher
in Newton Centre, Massachusetts**

For their help in clarifying the complexities of ancient Egyptian history and thought, the author wishes to thank the following persons associated with the Oriental Institute at the University of Chicago: Kathleen Picken, Joan Barghusen, and Lanny Bell, and also Peter Piccione, particularly for his information about the pharaoh "playing ball." For suggestions regarding folklore, thanks to Shahira Davezac and Hassan El-Shamy of Indiana University, and to Pamela Service for her reading of the manuscript.

Benchmark Books
Marshall Cavendish Corporation
99 White Plains Road
Tarrytown, New York 10591-9001

© Marshall Cavendish Corporation 1996

Library of Congress Cataloging-in-Publication Data

Marston, Elsa.
    The ancient Egyptians / by Elsa Marston.
        p.   cm.—(Cultures of the past)
      SUMMARY: Introduces the customs, important events, religions, and famous people of ancient Egypt and includes a time line of the Egyptian dynasties.
    ISBN 0-7614-0073-7
    1. Egypt—Civilization—To 332 B.C.—Juvenile literature. [1. Egypt—Civilization—To 332 B.C.] I. Title II. Series.
DT61.M34   1996
932—dc20   95-5664

Printed and bound in Italy

Book design by Carol Matsuyama
Photo research by Debbie Needleman

Front cover: Queen Nefertiti makes an offering to the gods in a tomb painting from the Valley of the Queens.
Back cover: The Alabaster Sphinx at Memphis, erected about 1450 B.C.E.

Photo Credits

Front cover and page 31: courtesy of Valley of the Queens, Thebes, Egypt/Giraudon/Bridgeman Art Library, London; back cover and page 69: courtesy of Bridgeman Art Library, London; pages 6, 20, 22, 24, 26, 30, 46, 52, 55 *(bottom)*, 59: Werner Forman/Art Resource, NY; page 7: Giza, Cairo/Giraudon/Bridgeman Art Library, London; pages 8, 11, 12, 19, 34, 36: Erich Lessing/Art Resource, NY; pages 10, 49, 63, 64: Envision/Michael J. Howell; page 13: The Metropolitan Museum of Art, Fletcher Fund, 1923; page 15: Karnak, Egypt/Giraudon/Bridgeman Art Library, London; page 17: Fitzwilliam Museum, University of Cambridge/Bridgeman Art Library, London; page 18: Louvre, Paris/Bridgeman Art Library, London; page 21: Envision/John Lampl; page 23: Index, Barcelona/Bridgeman Art Library, London; page 27: Valley of the Nobles, Thebes, Egypt/Giraudon/Bridgeman Art Library, London; pages 28, 66: Robert Caputo/AURORA; page 29: Dave Bartruff; page 35: Scala/Art Resource, NY; pages 38, 55 *(top)*, 60: British Museum, London/Bridgeman Art Library, London; pages 40, 48: Giraudon/Art Resource, NY; page 45: Tomb of Nakht, Thebes, Egypt/Giraudon/Bridgeman Art Library, London; page 50: Bridgeman/Art Resource, NY; Page 53: John Hillelson Agency/Brian Brake; page 56: Copyright British Museum; page 71: Envision/Henryk T. Kaiser.

CONTENTS

CHAPTER ONE

NATION OF THE NILE

Egypt's first great king, Narmer, threatens his defeated enemies with a weapon called a mace. This decorated palette, or flat stone used for grinding pigments, is the earliest known representation of an Egyptian ruler.

For thousands of years people have marveled at the Great Pyramids, the Sphinx, and the huge stone temples rising above the sands of Egypt. Who could have created such amazing monuments? And why? What secrets do they hold?

Not long ago, people finally began to find answers to these very questions. By uncovering ruins from the past and learning to read the ancient Egyptian language, explorers and scholars have unlocked some of the mysteries surrounding the people who created Egypt's age-old wonders. Many of the explorers' discoveries fill museums in Europe and the United States, bringing us face to face with the remains of a fascinating culture. But the ancient Egyptians left far more than objects to dazzle museum visitors. Just as fascinating as any museum treasure are the ideas that inspired the Egyptians' amazing accomplishments.

This book is about those ideas. We will look at the history, art, and everyday life of the ancient people who lived along the Nile River. But we will also explore how those people viewed the universe and their place in it—the beliefs that lay behind everything they did. As we understand the ancient Egyptians' ideas about the world, we will find the key to some of the secrets that have intrigued people for so long.

First, let's see how the great Egyptian civilization came into being, grew strong, and faded from glory.

The World's First State

In the entrance hall of the Egyptian Museum in Cairo stands a slab of black slate about the size and shape of a small shield. Carved on the tablet's smooth face is the image of a king named Narmer strik-

The Great Sphinx, with the head of the Old Kingdom ruler Khafre and the body of a powerful lion, rises dramatically over the Egyptian desert sands. Behind the Sphinx is the majestic pyramid of the king Khufu.

ing his enemies. The Narmer Palette, one of the museum's most important treasures, is believed to record the uniting of two kingdoms into one. Today we call that one united kingdom ancient Egypt, the first and longest-lasting nation-state in the world.

Like Egypt today, the country of ancient Egypt was mostly desert. As a home to living creatures, it would hardly exist at all without the Nile River. The longest river in the world, the mighty Nile flows north from deep in the African continent. In southern and middle Egypt it passes through a narrow valley carved through highlands; this region is called Upper Egypt or the Nile Valley.

The lush, fertile valley and islands that are watered by the Nile River look astonishingly different from the hot, dry, sandy highlands that surround them.

Coursing farther north, the Nile spreads out in several branches to meet the Mediterranean Sea. This low-lying northern region is called Lower Egypt or the Nile Delta. Ancient Egyptians called the entire country Kemet (KE-met), or Black Land, after the rich, dark soil deposited by the river in the Valley and Delta regions.

Around 3100 B.C.E.* Upper Egypt was united under a single king. Gradually the kingdom of Upper Egypt took over Lower Egypt, forming a vast single state. Egypt was divided into forty-two provinces, or nomes, run by hundreds of local governors but ruled by a single king. Under this strong, well-organized system, the state of Egypt flourished.

Ancient Egypt's history is usually organized around its kings or, more precisely, its dynasties—the powerful families who ruled for generation after generation. An Egyptian priest named Manetho (mah-NEE-thoh), who lived in the third century B.C.E., was the first to organize the history this way. Using records kept since the start of the unified state, Manetho divided the history of Egypt into the rule of thirty different dynasties. The ancient priest's history contains quite a few errors, but it is still the most useful framework for understanding Egypt's distant past.

The Early Dynasties

Egypt's First and Second Dynasties ruled the united country in the Early Dynastic Period, beginning around 3100 B.C.E. Kings of these dynasties built their capital at Memphis, at the fertile tip of the Nile Delta. To record events in their widespread kingdom—and to make sure all provinces kept up-to-date with their taxes—these early rulers devised a system of pictures and symbols that developed into Egypt's first written language.

Next came the Old Kingdom, or Pyramid Age, when the Third to Sixth Dynasties reigned. Life was good in the Old Kingdom. Egypt was at peace, and trade flourished. Mighty kings built the Great Pyramids, and sculptors and tomb painters created

*Many systems of dating have been used by different cultures throughout history. This series of books uses B.C.E. (Before Common Era) and C.E. (Common Era) instead of B.C. (Before Christ) and A.D. (Anno Domini) out of respect for the diversity of the world's peoples.

The Great Pyramids of Giza loom over drifting sands. Originally part of the royal tombs, these magnificent monuments are now part of the scenery in a Cairo suburb.

the finest art of Egypt's history. But the Sixth Dynasty's last king, Pepi II, ruled for ninety-four years—an incredibly long time in the days when most Egyptians died before age forty—and Egypt's government grew as tired and weak as its leader. When Pepi finally died, the government collapsed.

With no strong central government in control, the nomes claimed independence, and wars flared up between them. One dynasty quickly followed another. Strong rulers eventually emerged in two cities: Herakleopolis (he-rah-klee-OH-po-lis) in the north and Thebes in the south. Around 2040 B.C.E. the kings of Thebes defeated their northern rivals, and Egypt was united once again.

Two centuries of wealth and stability followed. From their capital at Thebes, the strong rulers of this Middle Kingdom expanded trade and conquered lands in Nubia—now part of Sudan—to the south. Many of the finest works of Egyptian literature were written, and kings once again began to build pyramids.

The ancient Egyptians prided themselves on their accurate portrayal of the world around them. Here an artist has worked hard to show the difference between two prisoners of war. The man on the left is from Nubia, south of Egypt, and the man on the right is probably from Syria.

But around 1650 B.C.E. a new threat to Egypt's ancient order arose.

For many years foreigners from Syria and Palestine to the east had been settling in the fertile Nile Delta. As Egypt's kings began to weaken under challenges from strong nobles and governors, these foreign "invaders," or Hyksos, grew in power. Around 1650 the Hyksos set up their own dynasty in northern Egypt, while the weak Egyptian kings clung to power in the south.

HIPPOS AND HYKSOS

One day, after many years of Hyksos rule, a messenger brought a strange command to King Sekenenre (se-ke-NEN-ray), the Egyptian ruler in Thebes. It was from King Apopi (ah-POH-pee), the Hyksos ruler in the Delta. Apopi complained that the "pool of hippopotami" in Thebes were bellowing so loudly they were keeping him awake at night. They would have to be done away with.

Hippos can bellow, all right, but could their bellowing really be heard in the Delta, several hundred miles away?

Sekenenre doubtless knew what to make of the mystery. King Apopi suspected that rebellion was brewing in Thebes, and he was making a veiled threat: "Keep it quiet down there—or else!" Sekenenre's answer was not to hush the hippos but to hit the Hyksos. He launched an invasion and his sons, Kamose and Ahmose, finally drove the Hyksos from Egypt. You can read about it in an exciting—though not totally accurate—novel called *Shadow Hawk*, by Andre Norton.

A hippopotamus wading among the plants and wildlife of the Nile River must have been a common sight in ancient Egypt. This sculpture of a hippopotamus, found in a tomb, has been decorated with drawings of a bird (on its back) and of papyrus and lotus blossoms.

The Hyksos left their subjects pretty much free to run their own affairs. But to the Egyptians, rule by even well-meaning foreigners was humiliating. After years of domination, the king at Thebes and his two sons went to war and succeeded in driving the Hyksos from Egypt.

The New Kingdom

Determined never again to let foreigners control Egypt, the kings of the Eighteenth Dynasty—first rulers of the New Kingdom—turned their attention eastward. They had two goals: to protect foreign trade routes and to subdue rising powers in the Middle East, especially the Hittite empire. Before long, Egypt could claim a rich and glorious empire of its own, stretching south to east from Nubia to the Euphrates River in Syria.

The rulers who built this great empire were the first to call themselves pharaoh (FAY-roh), meaning "great house." These pharaohs included several remarkable leaders. One of the most memorable was a woman. Hatshepsut (haht-SHEP-sut) at first ruled alongside her nephew Tuthmose (TUTH-mohs) III, who was just a child when he became king. But Hatshepsut soon declared herself king—not queen but king! After she had ruled capably for fifteen years, Tuthmose took back the throne. In an explosion of energy, he pushed the boundaries of Egypt to their farthest limits. A strong king and skillful general, Tuthmose III kept both his country and empire in order, until his death around 1430 B.C.E.

Another extraordinary New Kingdom ruler—perhaps the most extraordinary of all ancient Egypt's kings—was Akhenaton (ahk-NAH-ton), the "heretic king." Akhenaton shook up traditional politics and religion. He moved Egypt's capital from Thebes to a desolate site three hundred miles away, known today as Amarna, and there he built a splendid new city from scratch. At the same time he tried to create a new religion, based on the worship of one god instead of many.

Perhaps in response to those who thought that a woman could not rule well, Hatshepsut often appears in statues as a male pharaoh, complete with a man's body, clothing, and beard!

13

Akhenaton was a man of vision, but he was not a very effective leader. During his twenty-year reign, Egypt fell into disorder, and the empire started to crumble. On his death the young pharaoh Tutankhamen (toot-ahnk-AH-mun) moved the court back to Thebes, and after Tutankhamen's early death, the army general Horemheb (HOR-ehm-heb) reestablished order in the country.

Seti I, the first ruler of the Nineteenth Dynasty, restored order throughout Egypt's empire. His son was the famous pharaoh Ramses (RAHM-sees) II, the greatest builder of all Egypt's kings. Ramses II made an important treaty with the powerful Hittites, probably the first peace treaty in history.

The kings who followed Ramses II had to deal with a new threat—invaders known as the "Sea Peoples." Around 1100 B.C.E. many peoples of the eastern Mediterranean left their homelands, probably because of famine, and tried to build new homes through conquest. Ramses III succeeded in fighting off an invasion by Sea Peoples allied with forces from Libya, west of Egypt. But the reigns of Ramses II and III proved to be the late afternoon of Egypt's power. The eight pharaohs who followed also bore the name Ramses, but under their rule the name lost its glory. Foreign invaders continued to nibble away at Egypt's strength and empire. By the end of the New Kingdom in 1085 B.C.E., Egypt's government was divided and its vast empire had been lost.

Final Days

In the centuries of confused rule that followed the New Kingdom, Egypt's government grew weak and corrupt. Priests gained power until they rivaled and even dominated the pharaohs. Then rule passed to one set of foreigners after another.

A dynasty of kings originally from Libya held power in Lower Egypt. Then kings from Nubia moved north and eventually controlled enough land to set up their own dynasty. Next came the Assyrians from Mesopotamia (present-day Syria and Iraq). After winning control from the Nubians, the Assyrians appointed a governor from the Egyptian town of Sais (SAY-is) to run the country. The Saite (SAY-ait) governor soon turned on his masters and established his own dynasty.

In spite of invasions by the Sea Peoples, Ramses III managed to erect this immense, glorious monument to himself at Karnak.

The Saite pharaohs rebuilt trade and Egyptian pride. But the days of glory of this final line of strong Egyptian kings lasted just one hundred years. In 525 B.C.E., Persian armies claimed Egypt for their emperor. In 404 B.C.E., the Persians were forced to give up Egypt for a while. Their empire had become too large to manage. But they returned about sixty years later and reconquered.

15

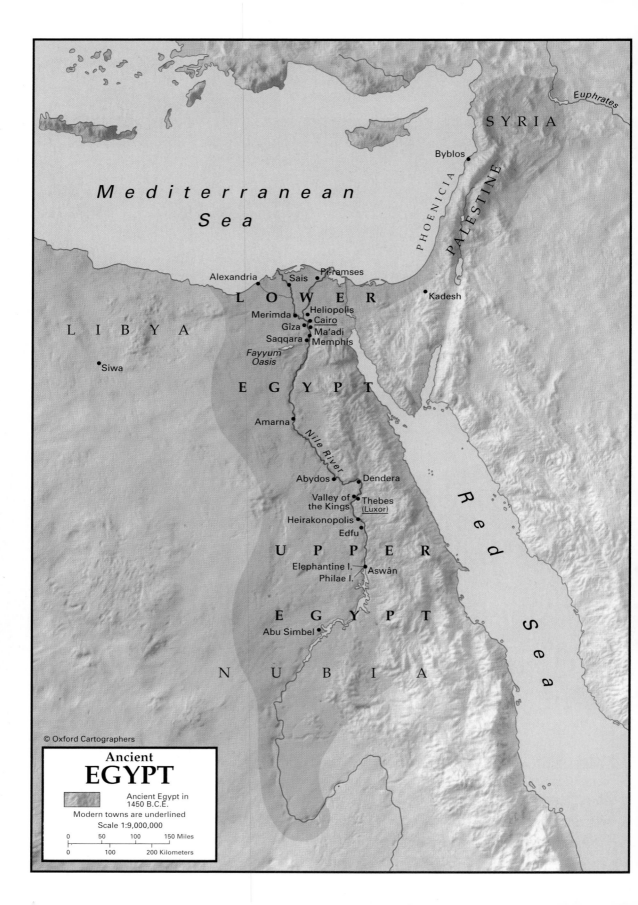

Euphrates

SYRIA

Byblos

PHOENICIA

PALESTINE

*Mediterranean
Sea*

Alexandria
Sais
Pi-ramses

L O W E R

Kadesh

Heliopolis
Merimda
<u>Cairo</u>
Giza
Ma'adi
Saqqara
Memphis

*Fayyum
Oasis*

L I B Y A

E G Y P T

Siwa

Nile River

Amarna

Abydos
Dendera

Valley of
the Kings
Thebes
<u>(Luxor)</u>

Heirakonopolis

Edfu

U P P E R

Elephantine I.
Philae I.
Aswân

E G Y P T

Abu Simbel

*Red
Sea*

N U B I A

© Oxford Cartographers

Ancient
EGYPT

Ancient Egypt in
1450 B.C.E.
Modern towns are underlined
Scale 1:9,000,000

| 0 | 50 | 100 | 150 Miles |

| 0 | 100 | | 200 Kilometers |

The Persians were harsh rulers, so the Egyptians were not unhappy when the ancient world's most famous conqueror, Alexander the Great, neared their borders. Alexander already had conquered Greece and much of the Persian empire when he reached the Nile in 332 B.C.E. During his nine-year reign, Alexander respected Egypt's culture and tried to blend Greek and Egyptian customs.

When Alexander died, his empire was divided, and Egypt came under the control of an officer in his army, Ptolemy (TOHL-u-mee). Ptolemaic (tohl-u-MAY-ik) rulers sat on Egypt's throne for the next three hundred years. The last and most famous of the Ptolemies, Cleopatra, was defeated by the Roman army in 30 B.C.E. and Egypt became part of the Roman Empire.

In time most Egyptians adopted the Christian religion, in a form called Coptic, and rule passed to the Byzantine Empire. The year 640 C.E. brought invasions by Muslim Arabs from the Arabian Peninsula. Their conquest in 642 marked the start of a brand-new era in Egyptian history.

During the Roman period in Egypt, the ancient Egyptian custom of mummification was still practiced. While the forms of the symbols had not changed greatly, the Roman influence is obvious in the lifelike portrait of the deceased.

17

CHAPTER TWO

THE THIRTY-CENTURY CIVILIZATION

The ancient Egyptians created beautiful objects for every part of their lives—and afterlives. This spoon, used to apply cosmetics, was carefully crafted from wood and shows a musician playing a lute.

For at least 150,000 years, during the Stone Age, nomadic peoples roamed the land that is now Egypt. There was much more rain then, and plenty of animal and plant life. As the climate grew drier, and as people learned to grow their own food and to raise animals, they settled in the fertile Nile Valley and the Delta.

Predynastic Egypt: Before the Kings

The three or four centuries just before Egypt became a unified state are called the Predynastic Period. In Lower Egypt there is little information about predynastic times, because the traces of that period are deeply buried. Thousands of years of flooding by the Nile have produced thick layers of silt and soil in the Delta.

A few communities have been excavated, however. At the western edge of the Delta are the well-preserved remains of a large village known as Merimda. From around 4900 to 4250 B.C.E., farmers lived there in small oval-shaped huts along "streets." They buried the dead very simply, with no grave goods or offerings, such as the food and valuable or useful objects that many ancient people believed a dead person would need in an afterlife.

A much richer town flourished at a site called Ma'adi (MAH-dee), just south of present-day Cairo. The people of that town were merchants, who prospered from trade with southwestern Asia. They were also the first Egyptians known to have worked with metal—copper from the Sinai Peninsula. Evidently they wanted to enjoy their wealth in *this* life, for their burials were simple, too.

The people in Upper Egypt, however, followed a very different lifestyle. Many prosperous communities grew up, based on farming; two of the most important are known today as Badari (bu-DAH-ree) and Naqada (nu-KAH-du). The fertile land in the Nile Valley was narrow, so there was plenty of desert close by—a good place to bury

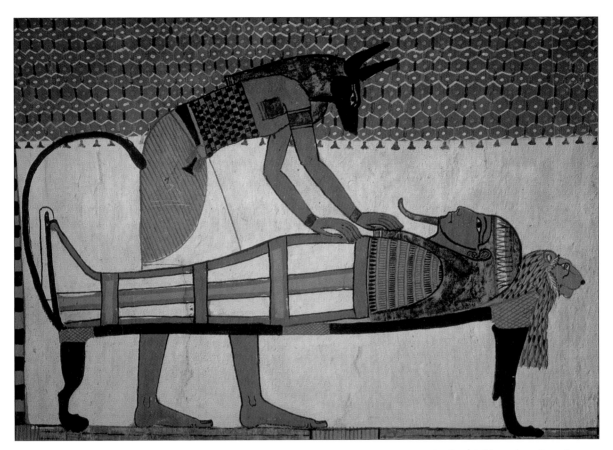

the dead. Well-preserved predynastic cemeteries have been found in the desert, and they tell a lot about the culture of these people.

Unlike the more northern communities, the Upper Egyptians *did* want fancy burials. Grave offerings included linen and leather clothing, carefully worked flint knives and blades, fine pottery, jewelry made of rare stones, ivory combs, copper tools and daggers, decorated slate palettes for grinding eyeshadow, and handsome stone vessels shaped by a drill. These burials, containing so many objects, indicate belief in an afterlife. They also reveal definite social differences: the rich were certainly getting richer.

Life in the Nile Valley became increasingly complex by around 3300 B.C.E. Because people wanted elaborate burials, whole industries grew up for preparing tombs and making expensive objects to be buried with the dead. Trade, especially for luxury goods such as rare stones to be used in jewelry, grew more important.

But this complex society could not have developed at all, were it not for the Nile River. Because Egypt had so little rain, the river was what made life possible. Every year the Nile overflowed

In this richly colored tomb painting, Anubis, the jackal-headed god of the dead, leans over the mummy of Sennutem, the owner of the tomb. The artist has realistically shown the elaborately decorated cloth hanging above the mummy, as well as his lion-headed bed.

Found in a First Dynasty tomb, this portion of a linen dress, with its elaborate pleats, may be one of the oldest garments in the world.

its banks, flooding the land and depositing another layer of fertile mud, which ensured another good year for crops. It also served as the primary means of communication and transportation. Still, the river had to be managed. Marshes were drained, irrigation dikes and canals constructed. Since farming by irrigation required people to work together cooperatively, they had to be well organized and directed. The need for good management increased the power of local chiefs, who took charge of controlling the waters. For example, on the carved stone head of a ceremonial war club, a predynastic ruler is shown opening a canal.

Other clues from this time have come down to us. They suggest that a foreign influence made itself felt throughout the land. Egyptians in both the Nile Valley and the Delta started using unusual designs for decoration, such as mythical beasts with entwined necks and clay pegs arranged artistically in walls. These ideas clearly came from Mesopotamia, though it's not certain just how they arrived—whether by direct trade or perhaps through traders from Syria.

Because of these foreign cultural influences, some scholars have suggested that a dynamic new people must have come to Egypt and led the drive to unify the country. Other scholars believe that the Upper Egyptians themselves brought about a unified state. It appears that they gradually dominated Lower Egypt through the spread of their rich, sophisticated Nile Valley culture—rather than through warfare. Even so, it probably wasn't an entirely peaceful change, since large numbers of stone war clubs have been found from this period.

Early Dynastic Egypt: The Shape of Everything to Come

A remarkable fact about ancient Egyptian culture is that it did not develop gradually during its three-thousand-year existence but took shape, to a large extent, right at the start. Most of the basic traits that were to mark the society appeared during the first two dynasties.

Elaborate, expensive burials became more and more important. Large cemeteries of royal tombs grew up at Abydos (u-BAI-dohs), which people believed to be the burial place of Osiris (oh-SAI-ris), one of the major gods. Farther north, nobles had their tombs built near the royal city of Memphis, at a desert site today called Saqqara (su-KAH-rah). During this time, the rules and characteristics of Egyptian art were formed, such as the stylized way of painting human beings, with the face and legs viewed from the side and the eye and the body seen from the front. Those were the "true" appearances of different parts of the face and figure, the ancient Egyptians believed. Highly skilled artisans also worked in stone, pottery, glass, copper, and gold.

Most important, the Egyptians learned to write. The earliest attempts that have been found were apparently just symbols on clay tags attached to royal grave offerings, but writing then developed quickly. Egypt's highly organized government needed an efficient way to keep records, in order to control and tax the whole country. Also, kings and nobles naturally wanted a permanent record that praised their deeds.

This beautiful hieroglyphic writing decorated a tomb. Ancient Egyptians believed that certain magical and religious writings could help the deceased on their journey through the afterlife.

Before long, therefore, hieroglyphic writing was being used for monuments and important documents. In this elegant but complicated system of "picture writing," small pictures and symbols served in two ways: they represented ideas and also spelled words phonetically. A simplified version, hieratic, was devised for more practical, everyday purposes. With the development of writing, ancient Egypt became a historical society, that is, its written records could be preserved as history.

Everything was set for the Egyptians' amazing display of energy that produced the Great Pyramids and other achievements of the Old Kingdom.

The Old Kingdom: Age of Pyramids

King Zoser (JOH-zer), the first ruler of the Third Dynasty, started it all. Up till his time, the mid-2600s B.C.E., even royal tombs had been simple boxlike structures, a form that today we call a mastaba (MAHS-tu-bu). Zoser's tomb began that way, but his architect, Imhotep (im-HOH-tep), added one layer after another until he had created the six-layered, 204-foot (62 meters)-high Step Pyramid. This impressive monument was surrounded by a vast complex of courtyards and shrines.

Imhotep's masterpiece was the first use of stone for monumental building. From then on, the ancient Egyptians almost always built their temples and tombs of stone, to last for eternity. Houses and other buildings—even palaces—were still made of mud brick, because they were only for *this* world.

Though other Third Dynasty kings also built pyramids, those of the Fourth Dynasty took pyramid building just about as far as it could go. The pyramid of King Khufu (KOO-foo), one of the three on the edge of the Giza Plateau known as the Great Pyramids, is the largest stone building ever constructed. The two slightly smaller pyramids of his successors, Khafre (KAH-fray) and Menkaure (men-KOW-ray), were built close by. Each had a temple a short distance below in the valley, a broad covered

More than four thousand years ago, wealthy Egyptians used furniture like this modern-looking bed and chair found in the tomb of Khufu's mother. The uncomfortable-looking object at the head of the bed is an Egyptian pillow—the sleeper's head would rest in the crescent at its top!

causeway leading up the side of the plateau, and another temple just in front of the pyramid.

Why were the ancient Egyptians so fascinated by the pyramid shape? Possibly, scholars think, because that structure was linked to worship of the sun god. The pyramid seems to point to the sun—and certainly the Great Pyramids' polished stone sides would have been dazzling in the sunlight. The purpose of the pyramid, though, was to protect the body of the dead king and perpetuate his memory.

It must have taken tremendous organization to carry out such ambitious projects. Furthermore, pyramids were expensive. To pay for his tomb and temples, the king needed an efficient tax system, which was enforced by the provincial governors. Though the people were taxed heavily, they probably considered the project worthwhile because, they believed, their king was divine. The pyramids

BREAD FOR THE PYRAMID BUILDERS

How did those thousands of Egyptian peasants live while they were building the Great Pyramids? Not far from the Sphinx, archaeologists have recently discovered evidence of the workers' daily life. A bakery was found by accident—by a bulldozer.

Ancient Egyptians baked their bread, of barley flour, in heated pottery molds that look something like flowerpots. Beer was made from the same kind of dough, which was allowed to ferment until alcoholic. Since bread and beer were staples of Egyptian diet, the industries of baking, brewing, and pottery making went together. At large projects such as construction of pyramids, the government evidently conducted the whole business, distributing the bread and beer to the workers.

Though the Egyptians loved their beer and drank a lot of it, their bread may have caused them more trouble. Made of flour ground between stones, it contained grit—which wore down people's teeth. Many Egyptians, whether lowly pyramid workers or wealthy nobles, suffered from poor teeth because of the bread they ate.

Here is a nineteenth-century artist's vision of the building of a great pyramid. Experts now believe that the ancient Egyptians hauled the enormous stones from the quarries and dragged them up the ramps without the help of wheels.

were *not* built by slaves. Rather, the work crews were ordinary Egyptians, who had free time during the flood season, when they could not work their fields. Thus the pyramid complexes were really like huge public works, and they helped unify the country.

The Old Kingdom, especially the Fourth Dynasty, shone with confidence. Besides monumental architecture, tomb painting flourished at this time, as did sculpture. Khafre alone had at least 112 large statues carved for his temples—not to mention the Great Sphinx! Never in all of ancient Egypt's history did artists produce more beautiful work. Even today the paintings and statues speak to us of a splendidly self-assured people.

Statues of couples and entire families are common in the Old Kingdom. Here a dwarf named Seneb appears with his wife and children. Notice the way the Egyptian artist colors male figures brownish red, and females a lighter yellowish color.

The Middle Kingdom:
A Better Society After Bitter Years

We get a radically different picture, however, during the First Intermediate Period, starting in the mid-2100s B.C.E. The pessimistic literature of this time described a society "turned upside down": brothers fought against each other, nothing of value lasted, and servant girls talked back. Though artisans found employment in the provincial towns after the country split up, artwork was generally poor.

Then, after 2040 B.C.E., peace and prosperity were restored under the strong rulers of the Middle Kingdom. Most Egyptians were hardworking peasants, for the country had long been an agricultural society; but now emphasis was placed on making it a *good* society as well. The best literature comes from this time, including epic tales, "wisdom texts" full of advice about the proper way to live and to do one's job, and even passionate love poetry.

The kings started to build pyramids again. In Faiyum oasis,

THE STORY OF SINUHE

This tale, from the Middle Kingdom, is one of the best-known stories of Egyptian literature. It takes place in the twentieth century B.C.E.

As a young man, the courtier Sinuhe (SIN-oo-ay) accompanies Prince Senwosret on a military campaign against the Libyans, to the west of Egypt. While there, the prince receives word that his father, the king, has suddenly—and mysteriously—died. In all haste, Senwosret returns alone to Egypt. Soon afterward, Sinuhe happens to overhear a secretive conversation, which greatly alarms him. He runs away—all the way to western Asia. There, weak with thirst, he is given shelter by a tribal chieftain.

Sinuhe is summoned by the Asian ruler, who asks why he left Egypt. Explaining about the king's sudden death, Sinuhe insists that he was in no way involved—he just took fright and fled. He proclaims his loyalty to the new king of Egypt, Senwosret. This satisfies the ruler, who then invites Sinuhe to stay in Asia. Sinuhe is given some good land and settles down. With a wife and children, he lives very well indeed for many years.

As he grows older, however, Sinuhe is not happy. His heart still lies in Egypt, and he dreads the thought of dying in a foreign land. Finally he writes to Senwosret, pleading to be allowed to return. Senwosret answers promptly, urging him to come home and assuring him that he was never under any suspicion whatever. The king adds, "You shall not be put in a sheepskin and a mound made over you," in the manner of barbaric Asiatic burials.

So Sinuhe says good-bye to the Asiatics who had been so kind to him and returns to Egypt. He is greeted with open arms by the king, and with glad shouts by the queen and their children, who apparently had missed him sorely all those years.

That is the story of Sinuhe. We never know why he took flight in the first place. Did he possibly know something about an assassination plot against the old king? That's the mystery. Anyway, whatever Sinuhe's *untold* story, his longing for Egypt comes across movingly—as does the extraordinary compassion of the king.

for example, King Senwosret (sen-WOS-ret) II had a whole town carefully designed and laid out next to his pyramid. He moved his court there, making it the capital of the country for a while, and most of the residents probably worked on the pyramid complex.

Life was good, especially for the wealthy. We can see this from the tomb paintings, which show many daily activities, along with the marshes and wheat fields of river and farm. Paintings in royal tombs were solemn and religious, but nobles and high government officials had more freedom in choosing the scenes to be painted on their tomb walls. Other Middle Kingdom objects too, such as jewelry, are among the most beautiful ever found in Egypt.

In addition to beautiful jewelry and elaborate paintings, Middle Kingdom tombs also contained miniature sculptures of the tomb owners in their everyday lives. Here the deceased appears under the canopy on this tiny boat, attended by his servants.

But then came the troubled Second Intermediate Period and, around 1650 B.C.E., that humiliating time when Egypt was ruled by the hated Hyksos. What we know about the Hyksos from the Egyptians is unflattering—perhaps unfairly so. In fact, the Hyksos had become quite Egyptianized, having adopted the language, customs, and religion of the country. Local Egyptian officials were given a free hand, and life seems to have gone on quite peacefully. Moreover, Egypt's technology, which had been backward compared with advances made by other peoples of the region, gained a lot from the Hyksos. Egyptians learned to use the horse and chariot, a much improved bow, bronze weapons—plus a better loom and some new musical instruments.

After the Hyksos had been driven out, a change came in the Egyptians' way of thinking. Up till this point they had preferred to stay within their borders, except for trading expeditions and occasional military campaigns. Isolated and protected by the harsh desert on both sides of the Nile Valley, they had a self-contained, inward-looking society—and they had no doubt that Egyptians were the greatest people in the world. Now, however, they took on a new worldview, one of conquest and expansion. Equipped with their war chariots and fired up by ambitious, dynamic kings, they set out to create an empire for themselves.

The New Kingdom: Age of Empire

The conquered lands—from Nubia to the Euphrates River in Syria—were left in the hands of their own rulers. They did, however, have to pay tribute to their Egyptian overlords. Thus empire brought great rewards to Egypt, which became fabulously wealthy. Tribute, spoils of war, and luxury goods poured into the country, especially the capital city of Thebes. The kings built and enlarged awe-inspiring monuments, such as the temples at Thebes that we know today as Karnak and Luxor. This was the time of Egypt's most flamboyant power and glory.

Tuthmose III, who seems to have been clever and resourceful, demanded that the rulers of subject lands send their brothers and sons to live in Egypt. The boys were hostages, of course, but they were also well educated in Egyptian culture, so that they would feel

An elegant couple enjoys the music of a harpist in a tomb painting from Thebes.

loyal to Egypt in the future. Meanwhile, Egyptian towns bustled with all sorts of foreigners: ambassadors, visiting royalty, merchants, sailors, captives of war. They introduced new ideas, customs, and art styles. Egypt was now a cosmopolitan world leader.

Besides the change in Egypt's outlook on the world, its kings broke with the past in another interesting way. They did not display their wealth and power by building bigger and better pyramids. Apparently they had at last realized that large, conspicuous tombs might not be the best way to preserve their riches for the next world. Therefore, they went to the other extreme and chose a secret location: the desolate cliffs west of Thebes. As time went by, the desert ravines and cliffsides were riddled with carefully concealed tombs, creating a vast necropolis, or "city" of the dead. Today we call this royal burial place the Valley of the Kings. (The Valley of the Queens is nearby.) The skilled workers and artists who made the tombs lived in a special village in a barren valley close by, today called Deir el-Medina (dayr el-me-DEE-nu).

These rock chambers, even though not meant to be seen, were fantastic tombs, their walls covered with spectacular paintings.

The ancient Egyptians believed that the sun entered the underworld every night in the desert west of the Nile River. Here in the wasteland of the Valley of the Kings, the New Kingdom pharaohs created elaborate but secret tombs.

This exquisitely decorated gold sarcophagus bears the image of the handsome young king Tutankhamen.

Some stretch for long distances into the heart of the cliffs. To judge from Tutankhamen's tomb, the only king's tomb discovered with all its riches, they were jam-packed with massive sarcophaguses (coffins), gold, treasure, and offerings of all sorts. Actually, the tomb of Tutankhamen, who died suddenly and quite young, gives us just a hint. The burials of important, long-lived kings must have been fabulous beyond our imagining.

Heresy—or the Dawn of a New Faith?

Akhenaton, more than any other king in ancient Egypt's long history, challenged the nation's age-old customs. Because he seems to have had such an idealistic vision, he appeals to people today and has inspired many romantic historical novels and movies. He is even sometimes described as the first ancient thinker to accept monotheism, the belief in one God.

The truth about him, though, is not so simple. What Akhenaton did was to single out, from all the Egyptian gods, only one god to be worshiped. The god he chose was a certain form of the sun god, called Aton (AH-tun). The king wrote hymns about the sun's goodness toward all the world—but he may also have thought Aton's goodness was meant especially for him and his family, something like a private religion. In fact, he expected to be worshiped as a god himself, almost Aton's equal.

Akhenaton did not just sit around thinking beautiful thoughts with his beautiful wife, the celebrated Nefertiti (ne-fer-TEE-tee), whose sculpted portrait is so well known. As soon as he became king, Akhenaton began building on a grand scale—huge temples, luxurious palaces, and a whole new city. He also started a radically different style in art. Akhenaton and his family were portrayed in casual, affectionate poses—quite different from the formal, "godlike" ways in which kings had always been represented before.

Meanwhile, Akhenaton prohibited worship of gods other than Aton. He ordered temples to be closed and statues broken, especially those of the chief god, Amun (AH-mun). The king's actions naturally made the powerful priests of Amun furious. Nor were the Egyptian people very keen on the new religion. After Akhenaton's death, the cult of Aton was soon dropped and Amun was restored as the top god. Akhenaton's temples, palaces, and city were totally destroyed

Although the stone is worn, this scene captures the playfulness of Akhenaton, his wife, and three daughters basking in the rays of the sun god, Aton. Mummies of adults and children have shown us that the long, odd shape of the heads, which was considered a sign of beauty in this period, was achieved by tightly binding the heads of children from a very young age.

Wearing an elaborate and very heavy-looking headdress, Queen Nefertiti raises an offering to the gods.

by the former army general King Horemheb. Henceforth, anyone who dared to speak of Akhenaton at all had to refer to him as "that criminal" or "the heretic."

By the Nineteenth Dynasty, Akhenaton was quite forgotten and the pharaohs were ready for military action again. Ramses II's triumphs in war were not so spectacular as he wanted people to think—but he made up for any shortcomings by advertising on a grand scale. All up and down the country he built immense temples and gargantuan statues of himself. During his reign of sixty-seven years (approximately 1290 to 1224 B.C.E.), he must have kept whole armies of sculptors busy. He also established a magnificent new capital (as new dynasties often did) at his hometown in the Delta, Piramses (pi-RAHM-sees).

The last pharaoh to promote himself with such enthusiasm was Ramses III, in the first half of the 1100s B.C.E. His large temple, known as Medinet Habu (me-DEE-net HAH-boo), is one of the dramatic sights near Luxor. On the walls exciting scenes—including a sea battle—boast of Ramses III's triumphs over enemies.

The Fading of Ancient Egypt

As Egypt's political power dwindled after Ramses III, the cultural splendor that had dazzled the ancient world began to dim. Egyptians kept up the traditional religion and the customs and beliefs, but some of the sparkle had gone out of life. Perhaps it was the price of success: the superstate of the empire required too much regimentation and conformity. The confident attitude of the Old and Middle Kingdoms, when capable men of modest background could rise in the world, was gone. Society became more and more rigid, obsessed with religious rules, afraid to change and innovate. The priesthood kept a strong hold over both the king and the people.

For the most part, the art and architecture of the last dynasties were stiff, clumsy copies of the old styles. Egyptians enjoyed periods of prosperity, but literature from this time suggests that much of the former joy in life had dimmed. There were some attempts to revive the past, such as the strange-looking pyramids that the Nubian kings (late 700s and 600s B.C.E.) built in their own country. Also, the Saite pharaohs (664–525 B.C.E.) did much to renew the cultural glory of Egypt. Yet at the same time, the Saites encouraged the growth of foreign cultures in Egypt by depending on mercenary troops from other places, especially Greeks.

When Alexander took over Egypt from the Persians in 332 B.C.E., the Egyptians were delighted. Although he had a vision of developing a universal, harmonious culture, he respected the Egyptians and tried to fit Greek rule into their civilization. Soon after his arrival, Alexander made a difficult trip to the distant oasis of Siwa (SEE-wah). There, at the temple of Amun, he was declared the son of the god, a divinity like the pharaohs.

A Subject Race

During the three hundred years of rule under Ptolemaic kings, the Greeks adopted many Egyptian customs, such as religious ideas and mummification. The Ptolemies were also great builders and constructed many large, important temples, including those at Dendera, Edfu, and Philae (FEE-lay), an island near Aswan (ahs-WAHN). By adopting Egyptian culture, however, the Greeks apparently did not want simply to become Egyptian but to strengthen their hold over the country. Though there was some intermarriage, generally the Greek population treated the Egyptians as a subject race.

Meanwhile, a remarkable new center of culture grew in the seaside city of Alexandria, which had been founded by Alexander himself. It attracted the most important scholars, historians, and scientists from all over the Mediterranean world, and they made great advances in knowledge and invention. The lighthouse of Alexandria, one of the Seven Wonders of the Ancient World, is said to have stood 400 feet (122 meters) high. The Library of Alexandria, too, was a marvel, until it burned in 47 B.C.E., destroying much of the literary heritage of the ancient and classical world.

All this intellectual and scientific progress, however, had almost nothing to do with Egypt. The culture of the ancient Egyptians now faded more rapidly, even though the Romans, too, adopted some of their religious practices. A few centuries later, no one could read the ancient writings that recorded Egypt's past. A door had closed, sealing the glories of ancient Egypt for centuries to come.

CHAPTER THREE

HOW THE ANCIENT EGYPTIANS SAW THEIR UNIVERSE

This sleek and mysterious cat represents the Egyptian goddess Bastet. The Egyptians had a special reverence for cats, and their mummified remains are often found near the temples of Bastet.

If the gods of ancient Egypt were to visit America today and happen to see kids impersonating them, as in *The Egypt Game* by Zilpha Keatley Snyder, would they be angry? Not very likely. The Egyptians' gods were just as self-confident as the Egyptians themselves. They would probably have expected to be admired everywhere.

Unlike the religions of Judaism, Christianity, and Islam, which were founded on messages that their followers believe came from God, most ancient religions simply developed over time. Ancient Egypt's religion was like that. Egyptians happily accepted new gods, all the while holding on to the old ones. The result, as the centuries went by, was a confused jumble of beliefs, haphazard and contradictory. The ancient Egyptians didn't mind, though; contradiction didn't bother them one bit.

There was no "one truth" in ancient Egyptian religion. Some scholars have argued that the many gods really represented *one* god with different appearances, but other researchers feel that the Egyptians accepted many different forms of divinity. For the Egyptians, the whole universe was alive, with divine powers everywhere. The gods provided a mystical bond between humans and the natural world, an enduring source of strength. They embodied religion for the ancient Egyptians—and life *was* religion.

The Egyptian belief system had three main aspects. These were the worship of gods, the role of the king, and belief in life after death.

A couple offers sacrifices before the god of the underworld, Osiris, who always appears black or green in paintings. The egg-shaped objects on the worshipers heads are lumps of solid perfume that gave off fragrance as they melted in the Egyptian heat.

Multitudes of Gods

Some of Egypt's many, many gods came from predynastic times, such as Set and Horus (HOR-us). Others were local, belonging to this town or that, or even borrowed from non-Egyptian peoples. As gods were welcomed into the Egyptian collection of deities, they sometimes blended with other gods. In that way they took on a mixture of characteristics and roles.

The chief deities were the cosmic gods, who stood for the power of natural forces, especially in the sky. The sun, which gives life, was most important. Ra, the sun god, was the king of gods and

The goodness of the sun streams down upon the royal family, who offer sacrifices to Ra, the sun god.

the creator. He was worshiped from the earliest dynasties onward. Some other important deities were Horus, the sky god; Thoth, the god of learning; Hathor (HAH-thor), the goddess of "all things feminine"; Ptah (tah), the god of creation and craftsmanship; Khnum (knoom), the potter who created humans; and Anubis (u-NYOO-bis), the protector of the dead.

The gods and goddesses were not abstract ideas but were like real persons. They were shown vividly in paintings, reliefs, and sculpture, each one with a special appearance. Osiris, King of the Other World, was colored green or black, symbolizing the fertility of the soil. Ma'at (MAH-aht), the goddess of justice, carried an ostrich feather, while Isis (AI-sis), the wife of Osiris, wore a throne-shaped crown. Ptah was depicted as a mummy.

Many deities had a human body and the head or some feature of a particular animal. For instance, Hathor was often shown with the ears and/or horns of a cow. Khnum had the head of a ram, and Thoth had the odd-looking head of a long-billed ibis. The goddess Bastet (BAHS-tet) sat with a cat's head on a female form, and Sekhmet (SEK-met), protector of the king, had the head of a lioness. Horus, the sky god, had a falcon's head, perhaps because the falcon could be seen soaring high in the sky; and Anubis had the head of a jackal, probably because jackals were frequent visitors to graveyards. The goddess who assisted in childbirth, Taweret (tu-WAYR-et), was a hippopotamus.

Each deity was associated with at least one special role or task and often several, even contradictory ones. Bastet, for example, was a goddess of love—and war. Min was a god of male fertility, the desert, and thunder. Set, the jealous brother of Osiris, was the "bad god"—but a full member of deity society. In fact, it was his job to travel every night in the solar boat with Ra. He was supposed to protect the sun god against the dragon of chaos, Apophis (ah-POH-fis).

Why did the ancient Egyptians need all these gods? We may find them strange—but to their worshipers they were very real and important. Perhaps the following explanation may help us understand:

Though the Egyptians, then as now, depended on the unceasing flow and the annual overflow of the Nile, the flood was not a sure thing. Sometimes it came late, or was too low to renew the soil's fertility and supply water for irrigation. Famine could follow. Sometimes, too, the flood might be too high—and destroy whole villages. Compared with neighboring arid lands, where different peoples competed and fought to live, Egypt appeared blessed; but there was always uncertainty. Beneath their joy in life, the Egyptians seem to have felt fear. Chaos continually threatened, they believed, and might strike if the gods did not keep the world on track. And it was up to humans to keep the deities contented and strong.

ANIMAL GODS

Did the ancient Egyptians really worship animals? This is a particularly puzzling question about their religion. One possible explanation is that in very early times, people admired certain animals for special qualities, such as their strength or protectiveness. In some cases they may have hoped to appease a dangerous animal, such as the lion or the crocodile, by making it a god or goddess. Another idea is that animals were part of the eternal, unchanging force of nature and, in that sense, divine.

Why, though, did most animal gods have human bodies? Perhaps because animals, as such, could not communicate with people and thus would not be totally satisfactory deities. Therefore, the Egyptians may have given the gods animal heads (the most easily identifiable part) along with human bodies—since they believed that the heart was the organ of intellect. In this way, there could be communication between the gods and humans.

In addition certain animals were considered sacred, especially in the centuries when Egypt's culture was waning and foreign influence was increasing. Encouraged by the priests as distinctively Egyptian, some strange animal cults became popular. Huge numbers of mummified cats and ibises have been found, and even mummified crocodiles. In Saqqara there is an enormous stone tomb for the embalmed bodies of sacred bulls, who represented the god Ptah.

The Egyptians worked hard to make sure their gods were happy. The deities, they thought, had the same basic needs as people. In a society that greatly valued the family, the gods were married and had children. They needed homes where they could live peacefully and comfortably, so the Egyptians gave them homes—the temples. Not only did the deities receive offerings in the temples, but they were cared for like human beings. The priests would go through the daily ceremonies of getting the god's statue up in the morning, bathing and dressing it, presenting important visitors to it, providing it with good meals, and putting it to bed again at night.

In addition, the gods were treated to public festivals. The most important festival in Thebes, called Opet, lasted for twenty-four days. It honored the marriage of the chief god, Amun, and Mut (rhymes with "put"), the vulture-headed mother goddess. Priests

In this painting of a festival, perhaps for a harvest goddess, two families are shown hunting fowl in a dense papyrus marsh. The hunter on the left and his young son are carrying weapons called "throwing sticks."

carried boats containing the two deities' statues from the Temple of Amun (Karnak) to Luxor Temple. At both temples wall reliefs still show the processions and the excited crowds along the way.

The major gods were well taken care of by the priests. Ordinary people, however, seem to have felt closer to more homey deities, such as local gods or even personal gods that individuals could choose for themselves. Probably most homes had shrines for these gods. A popularity contest would doubtless have been won by Bes, a squat, ugly, naked, but kind little god. He especially looked after women and children, and his job description included happy marriage, dance, and good times.

Mythology: How the World Began, and Other Stories

Like most cultures, the Egyptians had creation myths that explained the origin of the world. The main myth may have been inspired by the sight of fertile land emerging from water each year as the Nile flood receded. This is how the world—that is, Egypt—came to be:

In the beginning was Nun (noon), the formless waters of the underworld, representing chaos. The creator god, Ra-Atum (rah-ah-TOOM), was there all by himself. Needing a place to stand, he first created a small mound of dry land in the midst of the waters. Then, from his own body, he created Shu (shoo), the god of air, and Tefnut (TEF-nut), the goddess of moisture. These two gave birth to the earth god, Geb, and the sky goddess, Nut (rhymes with "put"). From the union of Geb and Nut came four more gods: Osiris, Isis, Set, and Nephthys (NEF-this). This first family eventually created all the other gods.

Humans, on the other hand, were made more or less by accident. When Shu and Tefnut, the first children of Ra-Atum, were still young, the god's Eye—the sun—detached itself from his head and went to look after them. Ra-Atum naturally had to make another eye for himself. The original Eye, returning, was angry to find its place taken. It scolded Ra-Atum. The creator god wept, and his tears became human beings. To appease the Eye, Ra-Atum turned it into a serpent, which he put on his forehead as a protector. Then, at long last, he got down to the business of creating the rest of the world.

Shu, the god of the air, holds up Nut, the goddess of the sky. Below them is the dark-skinned Geb, god of the dark, rich earth. This picture tells the story of the separation of earth and sky.

This mythology grew up in a town later called Heliopolis (HEE-lee-o-pol-is), one of the oldest towns devoted to worship of the sun god. At Memphis, there was a somewhat different creation myth. In this story the god Ptah, representing the power in the earth, emerged even earlier than Ra-Atum. It was Ptah who created the gods and the world—not just by performing certain actions but by *intending* and *speaking*. In other words, he had a plan.

The most famous Egyptian myth is that of Osiris. The son of the earth god in that original family, Osiris ruled the world and taught human beings agriculture and civilization. His brother Set grew jealous and wanted the throne. Set killed Osiris, cut up his body, and scattered the pieces all over Egypt.

Isis, the loyal and loving wife of Osiris, searched for him high and low. At last she found all the parts of his body and put them together again by magic. Osiris revived enough to father a child. Then he left this world for good and became king of the Other World. The child of Isis and Osiris was named Horus. To protect him from his uncle Set, Isis brought him up in the marshes. When Horus reached manhood, he overcame Set and took his rightful

place as king of Egypt and of the rest of the earth.

The story has many universal themes: jealousy and violence, devotion, revenge—and family values. In addition, Osiris symbolizes rebirth: the revival of life each spring and the continuation of life after death for humans. We also find in this myth the basic Egyptian belief that *ma'at*—correctness, justice, order—must prevail.

The Egyptians had an earthy sense of humor from which even the gods and goddesses were not spared. The following story is a good example.

Ra, king of the gods, having grown old and a bit cranky, suspected human beings of plotting against him. He asked Sekhmet, the lioness goddess, to punish humankind. Sekhmet threw herself into the job with such enthusiasm that the desert was soon littered with dead bodies. Ra decided he must stop her before she wiped out humankind altogether.

Hitting upon a clever plan, he sent messengers to the island of Elephantine (at Aswan) to bring back large quantities of red ocher, a reddish earth. He added the red ocher to a freshly brewed batch of beer, which produced beer that looked like blood—seven thousand jars of it. Ra had all the beer poured out onto the fields at night. Next morning Sekhmet found a flood of what she thought was human blood. Delighted, she first admired her reflection, then took a good drink. The "blood" proved to be even better than she'd expected. She drank until she was quite intoxicated—and completely forgot about killing any more people. The human race was saved by seven thousand jars of red beer.

This story is also told of Hathor. The goddess of love, family, music, and mirrors, Hathor sometimes was bloodthirsty, too—an example of how contradictory the gods could be.

The King, a God on Earth

Ancient Egyptians had many gods to worship, but one dominated the lives of everyone: the king. From the start of unified Egypt, the king was regarded as divine. Because of the challenge of holding together two lands as different as the Delta and the Nile Valley, the idea of a sacred ruler appears to have been a wise political move. A king who was a god himself could have absolute power and would command the people's complete loyalty.

Throughout ancient Egypt's history, the fact that the ruler was king of the Two Lands was never forgotten. His crown, for instance, symbolized the unification. It combined the crown of Upper Egypt and that of Lower Egypt into one very tall piece of headgear. Later the cobra, symbol of the north, and the vulture, signifying the south, were added to the crown, to protect the king.

Every king, upon taking office, became identified with Horus, son of Osiris. Occasionally a king claimed that his parents were divine. In an inscription on a temple wall he would state that the sun god had visited his mother disguised as her husband and given her a child—himself.

Since it was unthinkable for a woman to be king, Hatshepsut proclaimed that she was actually the daughter of Amun and thus qualified for the job. Her successor, Tuthmose III, went her one better. He declared that one day when he, still a boy, was performing priestly duties, the statue of Amun moved under its own power until it stood directly before him and honored him as the future king. And it could have happened. Priests knew how to make startling things happen—or appear to happen.

All-powerful and all-knowing, like Horus, the Egyptian king was responsible for *everything*. In effect, he *was* Egypt and Egypt was his. His first duty was to serve as head of the religion, the link between his people and the gods. Egypt relied on him to carry out his divine mission, for he was vital to both humans and deities.

The king was responsible for his people's welfare in a more practical sense as well. Each year he traveled many hundreds of miles back and forth between Memphis and Thebes and sometimes other capital cities, governing his country. Lawgiver, executive, and judge, he knew about and carried out every detail affecting the people's lives. Yet with all his awesome power, he was supposed to act with mercy and kindness. It was his ultimate job to maintain *ma'at*—order and justice.

The king's third main duty lay in protecting his people. As commander in chief of Egypt's military might, he defended the country from danger and, when it seemed like a good idea, extended Egypt's power over foreigners.

It was a big job for one man, even a divine man, and we shall see in the next chapter how he managed. Moreover, after his term on earth was finished, he took on another kingship. Egyptians believed that just as the sun god traveled in a boat across the sky from east to west every day, the dead king traveled in a solar boat

THE KING PLAYS BALL

Being king of Egypt was not *all* hard work. One of the rituals that the king performed was actually a sort of ball game. With a special stick, the king would hit softball-size, leather-covered balls to the priests, who would catch them. This was said to "gladden the heart" of the goddess, usually Hathor or Sekhmet.

Why did the goddess get such a kick out of seeing the king play "stickball"? Because the ball symbolized the evil eye of Apophis, who represented darkness and chaos. By striking away the evil eye, the king destroyed it and at the same time protected the eye of Ra, the sun god.

Even though the game was a religious ritual, there's no reason it couldn't have been fun as well. We can imagine the king and priests performing the ritual in the temple courtyard, with lots of running and shouting. That would gladden the heart of any goddess.

to the land of eternal life in the west. There he became one with Osiris, king of the Other World.

How do we know so much about Egyptian religion? The ancient texts the Egyptians left contained many myths and vivid descriptions of ceremonies and magic spells. Their tomb paintings and temple reliefs, which depict the gods, also reveal a lot about their religious beliefs. In addition, later visitors, especially Greeks, wrote about what they observed.

The Egyptian belief system differed from other ancient religions of the Mediterranean region in some interesting ways. There was none of the emphasis on sacrifice that characterized such religions as those of the Phoenicians and Hebrews. Nor were the gods, however powerful, quick to anger. They were quite human, in fact, and usually good-natured. A deity who was pleased with an offering would be very likely to grant a wish, people believed.

Another difference from other religions was that Egyptians had almost no interest in the idea of sin. Their religion did not stress a sense of guilt for wrongdoing. Nor, apparently, did it encourage much serious thought about the ultimate meaning of life. The belief system did, however, emphasize moral behavior, as we'll see in discussing the idea of afterlife here and, at greater length, in the next chapter.

Life Everlasting

From predynastic times, ancient Egyptians believed in a life after death. In some ways, they appear to have been obsessed with death, since they devoted so much energy to preparing tombs and preserving bodies. Indeed they *were* obsessed with death—but not in any morbid, or unwholesome, sense. Rather, they tried to deny death because they loved life so much. Life was so enjoyable they wished it to go on forever.

Therefore, the ancient Egyptians convinced themselves that death, however sad, was not an end to life. It was merely a change. People would continue to live after the death of their earthly bodies, and their lives in the Other World would be like their lives in this world—maybe better.

Of course they could see that the earthly body had to stay in the tomb—or the spot of desert that was the final resting place for

In this New Kingdom tomb painting, grapes are being picked from the vine, just as they would be in everyday life. The Ancient Egyptians loved life so much they wanted it to go on forever.

the poorest Egyptians. Each person, though, had a *ka,* a spiritual "double." The *ka* would make it possible for the person to enjoy immortality. Usually depicted as two arms raised in prayer, the *ka* can be described as a protector who helped the person along the right path in life. Probably the closest idea we have is the "guardian angel." But the *ka* seems to have played its most important role after the person's death, accompanying him or her to the Other World.

Each individual also possessed a *ba,* which can be described as something like the soul or spirit. It was depicted as a small bird with a human head. The *ba,* too, became active after death, leaving the tomb by day and returning at night. The body, *ka,* and *ba* together made up the dead person's identity for the next life.

Eternal life was not, however, an automatic reward. First the individual had to be judged worthy of immortality. In the presence of the gods Osiris, Thoth, and Anubis, the person's heart would be placed on one side of a balance and the feather of the goddess Ma'at on the other side. If the heart had been made heavy by wrongdoing and thus weighed more than the feather, the person would be devoured by a monster. But if the heart was light, as was apparently more often the case, he or she could proceed toward the Other World.

Ancient Egyptians believed that the heart—not the brain— was the organ for thought and intentions. We look at it differently, of course, but we share the idea that a clear conscience and a light heart go together.

Masters of Magic

Magic fascinated the ancient Egyptians. Like divinity, it played a big part in their understanding of the world. Their religion, in fact, was based on magic. Taking care of gods in the hope that they will grant one's wishes is basically a magical notion.

To the Egyptians, knowledge included a lot of magic. Since priests were the masters of knowledge, they were the most expert in performing magic spells. Probably they believed in much of what they did, but they also knew how to use magic to serve their own purposes. For example, the statues of gods "spoke," giving predictions and answers to questions, thanks to the priests' magic spells—and clever mechanisms.

Priests didn't have a monopoly on magic, though. Anyone could use spells in everyday life. Everyone also wore small objects,

This scene from the Book of the Dead *shows the* ba—*in the form of a bird with a human head—being reunited with the body of the deceased person.*

called amulets, for protection and good luck. Special amulets could cure: a person would pour water on them while uttering words of magic and then drink the water. Such charms were highly useful for travelers who might encounter snakes or scorpions.

The *Book of the Dead,* a large collection of magic spells, prayers, hymns, and myths, was intended to help the dead make their way to the Other World. The ominous-sounding name by which the collection is known today is misleading; the ancient Egyptians actually called it *Incantations for the Going-Out by Day.* At first these incantations (spells spoken or sung) were reserved for royalty and written inside Fifth and Sixth Dynasty pyramids. Later, similar texts were placed in the coffins of nobility. By New Kingdom times, the entire collection was available for everyone.

Even though the Egyptians made important strides in mathematics, medicine, and other fields that we would call scientific, they still clung to their belief in magic. For instance, an important Old Kingdom manuscript about medical knowledge contained a good understanding of the circulatory system—but also magic spells that would "change an old man into a youth of twenty"!

The Old Ways

One firm belief underlay everything else in the Egyptians' religion: the world must not change. People were sure that the old ways— beliefs, customs, rules, institutions—had been set down perfectly at the beginning of creation. There was thus no need for change; in fact, just the opposite. What had been handed down since time immemorial must be carefully preserved.

These basic ideas that we've been discussing started in the first dynasties, if not earlier, and provided a sturdy frame for the way Egyptians looked at their world. It is often said that ancient Egypt never changed, that it stayed the same, as if cast in an unbreakable mold. Of course there was some change and variation, probably more than we can detect today; but on the whole, that judgment makes sense. The Egyptians' great strength seems to have been their confidence that, as long as the gods were on the job, things would go on as before . . . even if it meant a certain monotony and, toward the end, stagnation.

CHAPTER FOUR

GODS AND ORDINARY PEOPLE

H ow did the ancient Egyptians' ideas about their gods, king, and the next world shape life in *this* world?

Living with the Gods

Since the gods took care of the world and needed the comfort of a good home, temples were essential in Egyptian communities. Actually, there were two sorts of temples: the funerary temple, part of a king's tomb complex, and the cult temple for a god or group of gods. The latter is what is described here.

The seated scribe in this statue from the Old Kingdom holds a papyrus scroll in his lap. His rigid posture and direct gaze make him appear as if he is listening intently for words to transcribe.

When allowed to enter the outer parts of the cult temple, ordinary people must have found the experience awesome. The deity's "house" was intended to overwhelm the viewer. Reliefs on the outside walls glorified the king; and inside, the walls and heavy columns were covered with reliefs and inscriptions. This artwork was not just for decoration: it was intended to make the temple come alive with magical power. Only a little light entered the temple, which made it seem even more mysterious. At the farthest end was the small, dark sanctuary where the god slept.

The temple was not only the deity's home but also a center for administrative and intellectual activity, including schools. Scribes, artists, even doctors worked there, and of course, the priests. In the Old and Middle Kingdoms, most of the priesthood was part-time. Men, and some women, served for a certain number of months each year. The New Kingdom, however, produced temples on such a grand scale that large staffs of professional priests were needed. The basic job of the priest was to take care of the deity, with endless daily ritual, and to manage the temple property.

Priests did not have to be particularly religious people, just willing to put up with a lot of rules, such as those for ritual purity. They and their families led comfortable lives; they received a share in the temple income and were excused from paying certain taxes. What's more, they ate very well indeed, as did everyone connected with the temple. All that fine food and drink left over from the deity's daily dinner would certainly not have been thrown out.

The temple provided employment for many other people as well. To build, beautify, and run a temple was costly. Income was reckoned mainly in agricultural produce, since money was not used in Egypt until the Greek period, and therefore the temple owned large estates. It also rented out land. In this way, all sorts of people directly or indirectly worked for temples: peasants, farm laborers, artisans, boatmen, weavers, hunters, and so forth. It's said that in the Nineteenth Dynasty, the Temple of Amun alone required the

For people living in small mud-brick houses, the grandeur and immense size of the royal temples at Luxor must have been astonishing. Even modern visitors are awed by the enormous statues and towering architecture.

work of 81,000 people! At that time, one-third of all the land that could be cultivated in Egypt belonged to the temples—and the Temple of Amun got the lion's share.

Though the gods' temples required a great deal of income and work from Egyptian society, in return they shaped and preserved Egypt's culture. By and large, priests were the educated men of ancient Egypt, and the temple served as a permanent place to keep written records. Furthermore, it was the priests who maintained knowledge of hieroglyphic and hieratic writing. When the last temples were closed and the priests disbanded, shortly before 400 C.E., the ancient Egyptian writing died out. With it went knowledge of Egypt's past . . . until the 1820s, when a young Frenchman named Champollion (shahm-POH-lee-ohn) managed to decipher the scripts on the Rosetta stone.

The Rosetta stone bore a decree of the pharaoh Ptolemy V in three scripts: hieroglyphic Egyptian, hieratic Egyptian, and Greek. Nineteenth-century scholars, well versed in Greek, were able to work backward from the Greek to decipher the Egyptian scripts.

While the priests preserved knowledge, however, they did not seek it with open, inquiring minds. Nor did they wish to advance learning for the practical use and enlightenment of humankind. The priests wanted to keep their knowledge secret, the better to enhance their own power—hardly a scientific attitude. When Egypt was in decline, it relied too much on its limited, rigid priestly knowledge. In a changing world, that was not enough.

We may wonder what religion meant for the ordinary Egyptians. The priests certainly did not minister to the people— they took care of the god. Nor was the temple meant to serve for community worship. The people saw their god only once a year, when the statue was taken outside the temple. Nonetheless, the people seem to have felt a strong connection with their gods, especially the local god of the town. The deities maintained order in the world, after all. They inspired confidence during good times and offered something to cling to in difficult times. People were loyal to their gods until the time of Christianity.

One more interesting fact about Egyptian religion: Despite their many deities, the Egyptians did not fall into the chaos of religious wars. To be sure, there were occasional religious/political clashes, such as that at Akhenaton's time. But on the whole, the people do not seem to have made some gods more powerful than others to a dangerous extent; nor, apparently, did they form "parties" that would lead to all-out, widespread fighting. The gods, and their followers, seem to have been admirably tolerant.

The Job of King

Even when the king was most powerful, he never had a completely free hand to do just as he wanted. He was not a tyrant or dictator, because he, too, was supposed to be governed by the age-old system of order laid down when the world began. He had to rule according to *ma'at:* authority based on justice. Moreover, the king had to follow all the rules and rituals set forth by the priesthood.

The king was still responsible for everything, though, including the waters of the Nile. Obviously he needed some help. Above all he depended on a capable vizier (vi-ZEER), the chief authority in the government. A large, educated group of people—a "civil

In this tomb painting, temple officials (at lower left) *are inspecting a herd of cattle that is being brought as payment.*

service"—actually ran the day-to-day affairs of the country.

The king's massive building projects in the Old Kingdom were paid for by income from estates located around the country, in much the same way that the temples were supported later. Toward the end of that period, however, the system worked against the power of the king. As central authority weakened, the officials in charge of these estates took advantage of the great wealth in their hands and pursued their own political ambitions.

Though the king was always regarded as a link between humans and the divine, his role changed from one period to another. He was at his most "godlike" during the Pyramid Age (the Old Kingdom). Every Egyptian, in theory, worked for the king, and the ordinary people seem to have labored on their god-king's tomb with some pride. In the pyramids, blocks have been found bearing ancient graffiti: "The Enduring Gang," "The Victorious Gang." Nobles and high officials, meanwhile, wanted their tombs as close as possible to the pyramid of their king, in hopes of sharing in his divinity.

Statues of the king, at this time, had to show him in ideal form, a man in perfect physical condition. Take, for example, the statue of King Khafre in the Egyptian Museum in Cairo. There sits a god-king, if ever there was one! Queens, too, were eternally slim and beautiful, just like the goddesses.

Idealized, youthful, and impossibly handsome, Khafre's closeness to the god Horus, here a falcon, proves his connection to the great gods.

In the Middle Kingdom, after the upheavals of the Intermediate Period, the king came down to earth somewhat. His responsibility for the welfare of his people was emphasized, as if he were a "good shepherd." Sometimes in ceremonies the king held a shepherd's crook to illustrate this role. Moreover, royal statues were no longer idealized. Some kings were presented looking like ordinary persons, middle-aged and careworn.

Then came the exciting days of the New Kingdom—and the ruler was transformed into a mighty warrior. To be sure, ever since Narmer and his famous palette, the king had been shown symbolically smiting his enemies. Now he had to do so in person. He was expected not just to send his troops off to fight but to lead the troops himself.

Of course, the way a king carried out his "worldly" roles depended on what he was like as an individual. Some, such as Tuthmose I, his grandson Tuthmose III, and Seti I, apparently loved to go charging into battle. Others, includ-

ing Hatshepsut and Amenhotep III, preferred to stay at home, building temples and palaces; and for Akhenaton, military adventure held no charm at all. Some kings showed their vigor by being superathletes. Tuthmose III, Amenhotep II, and Amenhotep III boasted that they could ride, shoot, row, and run better than any number of lesser men—and kill many more lions.

Even in the late centuries of ancient Egypt, when many of the rulers were weak, the king was still regarded as divine. What mattered to the Egyptians was that a king *behave* like a king, sticking to the old rules and ceremonies, performing the religious duties. Even the first two Persian kings tried deliberately to fit into the image of the proper king, ruling according to *ma'at* and building temples.

Undoubtedly, many people were all too aware of their kings' human weaknesses. Like the gods themselves, god-kings were sometimes poked fun at in humorous stories. Nonetheless, faith that their king was divine gave the Egyptians a feeling of security and enhanced their sense of specialness and superiority.

How to Achieve Immortality

In the Old Kingdom, only the king became united with Osiris in the Other World. The Middle Kingdom, however, brought some change in social and religious ideas, and it was decided that *everyone* had the right to become Osiris.

The heart, though, still had to be judged. How could an ordinary person face such an awesome trial?

We have seen something of the importance of *ma'at,* the eternal sense of order established at the beginning of the world. *Ma'at* was everybody's business, not just the gods' and the king's. Respect for *ma'at* was essential for both the individual and society.

The Egyptians took a keen interest in correct behavior. Naturally, people should keep to their station in life, they thought, and not try to overturn or undermine the social order. But people had rights, too. Justice was everyone's due, rich or poor, man or woman. The poor would probably have to be more persistent, but in theory, individuals should be treated fairly regardless of their status. A well-known story from the Middle Kingdom, *The Eloquent Peasant,* tells about a poor farmer who has been treated unfairly and

MUMMIES

Why did the ancient Egyptians mummify their dead? The procedure was an essential part of their belief in the afterlife. For a person to enjoy eternal life, his or her body had to be preserved. The *ka* needed a home base: the body.

The Egyptians probably got the idea by observing that desert sands would sometimes dry and preserve a body naturally. Then they learned how to mummify artificially. Though at first only the royal and rich had the privilege of being preserved, later almost everyone but the very poor expected to be mummified. There were different grades of mummification, from the quick, cheap job to the full seventy days' treatment for kings.

The first step in mummification was to take out most of the internal organs and preserve them. The heart was left in the body to be weighed by the gods; the brain, though, was discarded because it was not thought to be of any value. After being immersed for many days in a special kind of salt called natron, the body was treated with special ointments and finally wrapped carefully in long strips of linen. The mummification business was always a thriving one, and it lasted well into Roman times.

This sarcophagus, or coffin, of a priestess of the Twenty-First Dynasty has been opened to reveal the mummy it contains.

The mummified head of Nebara, chief of the royal stables under Tuthmose III

finally, after much skillful pleading in high places, gets his justice.

Scribes must have copied "wisdom texts" till their fingers were sore. Some of these writings about proper behavior were for officials; for instance, *Instructions for the Vizier* set forth clearly the many duties of the vizier and the correct manner in which these responsibilities should be carried out. Some texts sound like the sort of advice a business executive today might give a son or daughter: "If you're invited to dinner with your boss, laugh at his jokes." And some urged husbands to be nice to their wives.

To the Egyptians, the wisdom texts were not as obvious or as trivial as they may appear to us. True, they probably did not make ancient Egypt a perfect society. Yet the fact that people honored the wisdom literature century after century means that it preserved important ideals for them. The essential thing was that it helped in maintaining *ma'at*. Ordinary people could expect no divine guidance in leading their lives; only the king could expect this. Therefore, these texts, containing the wisdom of the ages, pointed the way to the good life.

But what if, despite this moral guidance, a person committed crimes—was a scoundrel, or a crook? How were such people regarded by their neighbors?

In the first place, ancient Egyptians tended not to think of wrongdoers as evil. Rather, someone guilty of bad actions was considered an ignorant person who must be corrected. A wrongdoer

In this scene from the Book of the Dead, *the dead man, named Hunefer, is led to judgment by the jackal-headed god Anubis. In the center, Anubis weighs Hunefer's heart on a balance with the feather of truth while ibis-headed Thoth records the answer. The "Heart-eater," part crocodile, part lion, and part hippo, seems disappointed that Hunefer has passed this trial and will be led by falcon-headed Horus to Osiris.*

who later tried to behave according to *ma'at* probably would not be doomed. Anyone who refused to reform, though, would not achieve immortality. His or her life was contrary to *ma'at,* and without *ma'at,* the afterlife was impossible. At the judgment, that person's heart would outweigh the feather.

There was a source of help for anyone worried about his or her fate: The *Book of the Dead,* the collection of incantations. Those wealthy enough to have a rock tomb would have religious texts painted on the walls. But anyone could have written prayers and spells tucked in with their mummy wrappings, along with many amulets. With this insurance policy in place, any Egyptian could face the trial.

Long before a person got that far in his or her journey to the everlasting life, however, other preparations had to be made. The tomb had to be readied, a process that took a lot of time and expense. The purpose of the tomb, besides housing the mummy, was to provide all the conditions that would enable the person to go on to the

new life. Daily food, drink, and clothing would be needed, and a funerary priest could be employed to do the necessary work.

There was another way to provide for the dead person's future needs. The walls of the tomb were covered with scenes appropriate for the life of the tomb owner: banquets with lots of food, music, and dancing girls; cheerful servants and workers in the fields and barnyards, baking bread, making wine, weaving, slaughtering cattle; family members and others whose company the deceased person would like to have.

To our eyes the paintings are colorful, lively, and even amusing. In a Sixth Dynasty tomb painting, a worker tries to help a cow give birth, bracing one foot against the cow's hind leg and pulling the calf's head. In a harvest scene, two little girls squabble and yank each other's hair. Many of the tomb paintings were done with great artistry. Others were obviously just slapped on, as if the artists couldn't wait to get out of that tomb deep underground.

"Life" in the Tomb

Whether beautiful or sloppy, though, the paintings were not art or mere decoration to the ancient Egyptians. They had a practical, vital purpose: to make the lives of the tomb's occupants more comfortable in the next world. After the proper ceremonies, the pictures would become "real." With this magical idea of substitution, therefore, the picture or model would take the place of the real person or thing, a sensible way to keep a tomb well supplied for eternity.

Statues also served as substitutes. The king equipped his tomb with plenty of statues of himself, and other persons had less elegant statues of themselves in their tombs. If something should happen to the mummified body, the *ka* and *ba* would still need a home. A statue of the dead person would work almost as well.

There was one thing the Egyptians did not want to repeat in the Other World—and that was hard work. In this life, in principle, every individual had to labor at times on public projects for the state, such as cleaning the canals or working in the fields. Nobody wanted to have to do *that* in the future, so they found a way to get around it. People put in their tombs at least one small figurine, called a *shabti* (SHAHB-tee). Its job was to carry out any pesky duties for which the individual might be called upon in the next kingdom.

This lively tomb painting shows the deceased, Nebamun, hunting birds with his family in a papyrus marsh. His daughter's hair is shaved with the "sidelocks of youth," indicating that she is fairly young. Nebamun's cat has already captured three birds.

Of the other objects placed in the tomb, some were items that the person had used and enjoyed, such as toys, games, cosmetics, weapons—even, in some cases, toilet seats. But many of the finest objects were new, made especially for the burial. As in predynastic times, therefore, tomb preparation and manufacture of costly objects were important industries in the country's economy.

The artists—painter, sculptor, goldsmith—were vital to Egyptian society, both present and future. It was through their work that people could hope for a pleasant life in the Other World. However talented, though, artists were really just technicians. They

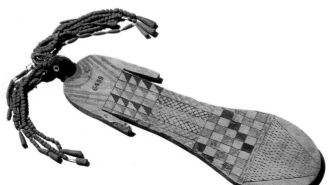

A child's doll was found in a tomb of the sixth century B.C.E.

worked in supervised teams, not very differently from those who had to dig the tomb out of the rock. Now we shall see why.

Preserving the Past

The artists had no desire to express themselves in their work or seek new creative styles. Their objective was simply to follow the rules that had been set in the first dynasties. The original ways of representing life in paint, stone, or wood were considered perfect and had to be preserved. Occasionally, there was some variation, particularly the radical changes decreed by Akhenaton, but the basic styles of Egyptian art remained the same. In the seventh and sixth centuries B.C.E., the Saite kings had their artists produce work as close as possible to that of the Old Kingdom, around two thousand years earlier.

Reverence for the past shaped Egyptian life in many other ways. As soon as writing was developed, the Egyptians started keeping records of their kings. The written record was highly important. The Egyptians made "paper" from papyrus, a plant that grows in marshy places. The long stems were cut in strips, laid flat in two layers at right angles, pressed together, and put in the sun to dry. This process created a smooth writing material in strips that could be stuck together and rolled up in scrolls—and it would last practically forever.

Ancient Egyptians greatly valued literacy. Many men of the privileged class—and a few women—learned to read and write. Hieroglyphic and even hieratic writing was not easy, however, so professional scribes were also needed. Government, religion, and society depended on scribes, who did all sorts of writing jobs, from keeping complicated official records to writing personal letters for others.

The sons of government officials and well-to-do merchants and artisans were sent to scribe school. Graduates would be sure to find good jobs and enjoy prestige. "Be a scribe!" was the earnest message of one of the wisdom texts that young students had to copy.

What about ambitious girls? Although there may have been a handful of women scribes, women were never employed in any

If you had been born during the Eighteenth Dynasty, around 1550 B.C.E., in ancient Egypt, your way of life would have been determined by the facts of your birth—whether you were a girl or a boy, free or slave, wealthy or poor. With this chart you can trace the course your life might have taken if you were a member of a well-to-do family in Memphis.

You were born in Memphis. . . .

As a Boy . . . **As a Girl . . .**

You live just outside the congested town, in a comfortable mud-brick house with courtyards, gardens, fish ponds, and a main hall for visitors. The house has flat roofs, where you like to sleep on hot nights. Your father is an official in charge of surveying land boundaries. Both of your parents give you much attention, and you play a lot with your brothers and sisters.

At age six you are sent to scribe school at the temple. There you learn mathematics and geometry and how to read and write in hieroglyphs.

▼

In your late teens you are appointed as a tax recorder, part of the enormous bureaucracy that runs the country for the king. Now you can start a household of your own; for many years, you've had your eye on the judge's pretty daughter.

▼

As a man your work gives you prestige and power, and your wife has given you several children. Ptah has responded well to your frequent offerings at his temple. Home life, with an occasional banquet for friends, is your greatest joy. You often take your children fishing. When your parents die, you provide for their mummification, ceremonies, and tomb offerings.

In childhood you and your brothers all wear your hair shaved off except for a small sidelock. While your brothers are at scribe school, you stay home and learn homemaking arts and weaving from your mother. There's no need for you to know how to read or write.

▼

In your midteens you marry—without any religious or legal ceremony. You simply agree to live with a man and make a home with him. Then you become mistress of the house and have as many children as possible, for that is the main purpose of marriage.

▼

As a wife you have servants to do most of the work. Like your brothers, you inherited land from your father, and you can earn some income of your own from that property. You serve as a temple musician, singing in the rituals. Your husband is not likely to want a divorce, or a second wife; but if he should, or if he should die, you can remarry.

In old age you lead an easy life, with your children and grandchildren living nearby. When you die, your eldest son takes care of your burial. You are quite confident that, accompanied by many amulets and prayers painted on your tomb walls, you will reach the Other World.

official or religious job that required literacy. Their work was in the home. They dealt with the present, while their educated husbands preserved the past.

The ancient Egyptians did not view life as struggle, nor as the pursuit of progress. Rather, life meant that harmony would somehow be maintained and the tried-and-true would go on. When bad things happened, they would be set right again when *ma'at* was restored. The rules had been laid down and needed only to be followed.

Undoing the Work of the Past

Yet there were contradictions in the Egyptians' reverence for the past. Normally, each king claimed that he followed in the footsteps of his father and all the kings who had gone before. At the same time, kings didn't hesitate to wipe out the memory of anyone they did not want to be associated with. The ancient Egyptians were almost as good at denying history as preserving it. They tried to blot out whole episodes that didn't "fit": the Hyksos, the rule of Hatshepsut, and of course that "criminal" Akhenaton. Other persons who had fallen from grace—even important ones such as viziers—became officially forgotten. Their banishment from memory was accomplished by defacing their tombs and scratching out their names on inscriptions in public places. So, when it was politically desirable, Egyptians could easily overlook the past.

There were more practical reasons, as well, that former royalty might be forgotten. Even in the early dynasties, kings sometimes used stones from previous kings' monuments to build their own. This sort of recycling went on, it seems, throughout ancient Egypt's history. The temples of Akhenaton and his successors were torn down not just to wipe out all memory of those kings but to provide material for new building. As for Ramses II, he had no shame whatever about chipping away the names of other kings on temples and statues, and substituting his own. For all their love of magic, the Egyptians were highly practical people. They didn't waste materials that could be used again—even if it sometimes meant undoing the work of the past.

And this brings us to tomb robbing. Tombs were robbed as soon as people started putting valuable things into them. No matter what plan was devised to baffle any intruder, the thieves always got

At the temple at Luxor, Ramses II "redecorated" an earlier temple built by Tuthmose III and Hatshepsut.

in. Everybody knew it, and tomb robbing must have been a very well organized, well paying, and, in a sense, practical occupation. But the contradiction is ironic. The ancient Egyptians believed that everyone would need provisions for life in the Other World—yet many Egyptians must have been quite willing to disregard that requirement. Their own needs or greed of the moment were more important than either preserving the past or ensuring someone else's future life.

CHAPTER FIVE

THE GIFTS OF THE PHARAOHS

What effect did ancient Egypt's culture have on other peoples? The civilizations of the Greeks and the Romans are said to have been strongly influenced by that of Egypt, and the whole ancient world must have been aware, at least, of the Egyptians' accomplishments. Let's have a closer look at the cultural gifts that pharaonic Egypt left to the world—then and now.

With sights as beautiful and mysterious as the sphinxes at Luxor Temple by moonlight, it is no wonder that the ancient Egyptians rarely felt compelled to wander far from home.

Ancient and Classical Times

During its long career as a superpower, ancient Egypt came in contact with many other peoples, such as the Minoan, Hittite, Mitanni, and Phoenician. Some of these peoples incorporated Egyptian gods and art styles into their societies. It's hard to tell, however, how much cultural impact Egypt had on other peoples or how long it lasted. This uncertainty comes largely from the very nature of Egyptian culture.

In the first place, the Egyptians did not particularly want to spread their culture. According to their ideas, they were far superior to all foreigners, and that was the way it should be. Why, then, try to make foreigners resemble them? If any foreigners wished to live in Egypt and adopt Egyptian ways, fine; Egyptian culture was not based on race. But there was no need to impose beliefs or win converts. Egyptian civilization was for the Egyptians.

Furthermore, Egyptians were not colonizers, because they did not like to leave home. They loved their own country and dreaded the awful fate of dying in some foreign land without the sort of burial that would ensure their afterlife. There were few small Egyptian colonies—for instance at Byblos, where the prized cedar wood from Lebanon was obtained. For the most part, though, Egyptians stayed home in the Black Land and left the day-to-day ruling of their empire to the local princes.

The Greeks, for their part, came to Egypt on their own initiative, as merchants, mercenary soldiers, and visitors. They were openly impressed by its wonders. What did they adopt of ancient Egyptian culture—and how did the two civilizations differ?

Greek sculpture, for example, at first looked like the straight-

forward, rigid pose of Egyptian statues, and the columns of Greek temples were inspired by Egyptian temples. Resemblances did not go much further, though, because the two peoples had different attitudes about life. Unlike the Egyptians, the Greeks saw no reason not to change. Before long, their styles in sculpture and architecture were developing in ways that were distinctively Greek.

These towering columns at Edfu remind us today of the ancient Egyptians' achievements in science and technology, architecture and art.

As for science and technology, let us first survey the Egyptians' accomplishments in this area. With their amazing technical skills in many crafts, the Egyptians could work equally well on an enormous scale, such as on colossal temples, and on a very small scale, such as on intricate jewelry. They worked out the first accurate calendar of 365 days. Their mastery of the mathematics, geometry, engineering, and even astronomy needed to build the Great Pyramids at Giza, for example, is astounding. Thanks to their experience with mummifying, they learned about anatomy and surgery, and they were renowned for medical practice. Much of this technology they contributed to the known world of their day.

The ancient Egyptians' pursuit of science, however, like their priests' secret knowledge, seems to have been limited. They did not seek understanding of the physical world for its own sake but for specific, practical purposes, such as hoisting huge stones into place. They believed that since the gods ruled the world, humans were not supposed to question or to probe but just to keep things going.

Again, the Greeks had a very different mentality. They accepted knowledge and science from the Egyptians, and with their open, inquiring minds, they went much further.

Likewise with history. The Egyptians carefully wrote down the record, the "what" and "when," but stopped there. The gods had made things happen, and that was enough. The Greeks admired the record keeping but, in contrast, also tried to explain the "why" and "how."

If it sounds as though the Greeks were much more advanced than the Egyptians, we must remember that the Greeks became acquainted with Egypt during its decline, from around 600 B.C.E. on. They could see the many marvelous reminders of its greatness. The Greeks were also awed by the air of mystery and secret knowledge with which the Egyptians now cloaked themselves. Even the great Greek historian Herodotus (he-ROH-du-tus), who visited Egypt in the fifth century B.C.E., swallowed a lot of nonsense. But they could not appreciate Egypt at its best. It was much too late for them to observe the creativity of Egypt's first two thousand years. Thus Greek visitors had mixed impressions of Egyptian culture. It seemed awe inspiring, yet strangely lifeless.

When the Romans took over Egypt in 30 B.C.E., like the Greeks they adopted some aspects of Egyptian religion. The cult of Isis especially appealed to them, and they carried the worship of this goddess to all parts of the Roman Empire. But when Rome became Christian in the fourth century C.E., the old deities suffered a deathblow.

To sum it up, ancient Egypt did not so much shape the Greek and Roman civilizations as provide a brilliant model. In its time, Egypt had realized extraordinary achievement and had tried to create a "good society." More than specific cultural influences, its example inspired the younger cultures to pursue their own distinctive development. And from those cultures came the foundation of Western civilization.

Echoes of the Past in Modern-day Egypt

Some visitors to Egypt feel disappointed that there is no obvious link between the Egypt of today and the fascinating Egypt of ancient times. The ancient Egyptians have totally vanished, they say.

Modern Egypt is, indeed, a very different place, with many social and economic problems. Naturally, too, the Egyptian people are molded by their Islamic culture (and, for some, by their Coptic

Christian religion) rather than by the long-dead culture of the ancient gods. If we look deeper and further, however, we may notice some links with the past.

Certain folk customs, still popular, have distant roots. On Muslim holy days, families go on cheerful picnics in cemeteries, something like the ancient practice of taking food to the dead. Another folk custom takes place in Luxor on a day honoring a Muslim saint. A small boat, kept in a medieval mosque built inside Luxor Temple, is carried through the streets in a lively, noisy procession—an echo of the Opet festival of ancient Thebes. As another example, when a theft occurs in a village, people carry a special water jug through the streets; a genie inside the jug is supposed to make the container point to the house of the thief. Ancient Egyptians did the same thing, using the statue of the god from the temple.

There may be other links with the past in the Egyptian character. Ancient Egyptians had a zest for life. So do present-day Egyptians, in spite of the hardships they face, such as overcrowding and poverty. Egyptians are known for their good humor, love of good times, and political jokes. They are friendly, talkative, kind, and hospitable; and they still radiate a certain self-confidence. Just as the ancient Egyptians piled their tables high with all sorts of delicious foods, today's Egyptians love to eat—and to share. At the same time, even though the educated people are very modernized, Egyptians still tend to be rather conservative, hesitant to make changes or take risks.

No, the people of ancient Egypt did not just vanish. Over the centuries, other racial and ethnic groups have settled in the land of the Nile—Africans, Greeks, Arabs, Syrians, Europeans; yet many people still have an "Egyptian" appearance that is distinctive throughout the Middle East. And, once in a while, you still see a face whose owner might have posed for a painting in an Old Kingdom tomb.

Ancient Egypt and the World Today

If you were to stop people on the street and ask what country they would most like to visit, probably at least half of them would say, "Egypt—the pyramids and temples and all that. It sounds so romantic."

The Alabaster Sphinx at Memphis. For centuries visitors to Egypt have been thrilled, astonished, and mystified by the ancient wonders they encountered in the desert sands.

As long as Egypt's monuments exist, they will surely attract visitors. Even people who have never seen the actual monuments are familiar with the art of ancient Egypt. Since the eighteenth century, Europeans and Americans have been fascinated by this art and eager to copy it in their own designs and building. Ancient Egyptian art and architecture still inspire popular taste in every-

69

EXPLORERS AND THIEVES

In 1798, Napoleon led a French army to seize control of Egypt. Not much came of that plan, but it did spark Europe's serious interest in ancient Egypt. Napoleon had taken with him a second small army, composed of scholars and artists; they busily studied and drew pictures of all the ancient monuments they could find.

Then began the plunder of Egypt's treasures. Europeans dug up everything within reach—statues, writings on papyrus, jewelry, temple reliefs—and took them away to museums and private collections.

The most energetic of the early explorers was Giovanni Battista Belzoni, who went to Egypt in 1815. A huge man, about six feet eight inches tall, Belzoni was the first to make his way inside the second of the Great Pyramids and to enter the famous temples at Abu Simbel, which had been nearly buried in sand. He collected sculpture, obelisks, and other objects for the British Museum in London, and met many a gruesome mummy.

While Belzoni admired the ancient art, he was really—like all the others—a sort of thief. At the same time, however, the ruler of Egypt wanted help from Europe in modernizing his country, so he was willing to let Europeans take what they wanted. For decades Egypt was looted, until some controls could be enforced. Today, no one—not even archaeologists—can legally take ancient objects out of Egypt.

thing from fashion to furniture, movie theaters to magazine covers. In the mid-1970s, the exhibit in the United States of just a few of Tutankhamen's treasures caused tremendous excitement and record-breaking lines at museums.

Look, too, at all the books—novels, nonfiction, photo-essays, romances, comics—about ancient Egypt, not to mention movies and TV specials. The land of the pharaohs has stirred the imaginations of writers since Shakespeare's time. All those strange deities, the kings who ruled as gods, the fascinating quest for life after death! They inspire all kinds of fiction and fantasy, as well as search for the "truth" of ancient Egypt.

For the last two hundred years, people have been combing Egypt for its treasures. Archaeologists are sure there is much more to be found. What most now seek are not just valuable decorative objects, such as gold jewelry and fine statues, but information about the life of ancient Egypt, the people and their society.

Egypt is such a rich and exciting field for research, it will keep Egyptologists busy for generations to come. Everyone will benefit

from their discoveries. We will learn more about the start of Western civilization and the world's first big nation-state. We'll understand better some parts of ancient Egypt's culture that seem strange to us. And we'll see even more ways in which the lives, experiences, and feelings of those long-ago people were not so different from ours today. Perhaps our continuing interest is the way the ancient Egyptians really did find immortality.

The glory of ancient Egypt can still be seen in modern sculpture. This sphinxlike image greets visitors from all over the world at the United States Customs House in New York City.

The Ancient Egyptians: A Time Line

B.C.E.

7000 — c. 7000–5000 B.C.E.
Paleolithic cultures

PREHISTORIC AND PREDYNASTIC

5000 — c. 5000–3100 B.C.E.
Neolithic cultures

DYNASTIC EGYPT

Early Dynastic Period **c. 3100–2686** B.C.E.
Dynasties I and II

Old Kingdom   **c. 2686–2181** B.C.E.
Dynasties III–VI

First Intermediate Period **c. 2181–2040** B.C.E.
Dynasties VII–X

Middle Kingdom **c. 2040–1795** B.C.E.
Dynasties XI and XII

Second Intermediate Period **c. 1795–1550** B.C.E.
Dynasties XIII–XVII; Hyksos rulers

New Kingdom **c. 1550–1085** B.C.E.
Dynasties XVIII–XX

Third Intermediate Period **c. 1085–664** B.C.E.
Dynasties XXI, XXII (Libyan),
XXIII–XXIV, and XXV (Nubian)

Late Period **664–332** B.C.E.
Dynasty XXVI (Saite, 664–525 B.C.E.)
Dynasty XXVII (Persian, 525–404 B.C.E.)
Dynasties XXVIII-XXX (404–343 B.C.E.)
Persian Reconquest (343–332 B.C.E.)

3100

2686

2181

2040

1550

332 — Greek (Ptolemaic) Period

30 — Roman Period
C.E.

395 — Byzantine Period

640 — Arab Conquest

NOTES ON NUMBERS AND NAMES

Ancient Egypt's dates cannot be given in precise, accurate terms. That's partly because its history began so very long ago, and partly because pharaonic history, though peaceful much of the time, was interrupted by periods of disorder, civil wars, overlapping dynasties, and foreign intrusions. Add to that the confusion caused by different ways of calculating the passage of time, and it's a wonder we know as much about those distant dates as we do. Although some dates seem to be generally accepted, most Egyptologists advise that a time line should be understood only as a general guide, not as firm information.

Another source of bewilderment for the reader is the great number of names in ancient Egyptian history. Actually the number of important individuals is not so large as it looks, because each ruler has at least two names: one Egyptian and the other a Greek form of that name. Both are used commonly in books. For example, Amenhotep and Amenophis are the same person, as are Khufu and Cheops, Khafre and Chephren, Hatshepsut and Hashepsowe, Tuthmose and Thuthmosis. Furthermore, because of the difficulties in transliterating hieroglyphs, the Egyptian names can be spelled in different ways.

In this book Egyptian names are used for the most part, in the form that seems most familiar and easy to pronounce. Even so, pronunciation is still a problem, because hieroglyphic writing did not include vowel sounds. We just have to guess at the way the words actually sounded.

GLOSSARY

amulet: a small object in the shape of a god, animal, or other symbol, believed to have magical powers of protection or good luck for the owner

bureaucracy: government run by officials in charge of different functions; these officials are organized by ranks and work by fixed rules

causeway: a raised road or processional route, usually over rough ground

chaos: a state of total confusion in which nothing is organized, meaningful, or in proper relationship to anything else

complex: an arrangement of buildings and structures, all related to each other for some purpose

cult: a particular system of religious worship and ritual, often focusing on a certain deity

divine: pertaining to God, or other gods, or some superhuman godlike power; sacred

dynasty: a powerful family whose leaders rule a country for more than one generation

Egyptologist: a person who studies ancient Egypt—its history, art, archaeology, writing, or other aspect

grave goods, grave offerings: objects and supplies, such as food, jewelry, and weapons, buried with the dead in the belief that they will be needed in an afterlife

heretic: a person who holds views that differ in important respects from the accepted beliefs of his or her religion

incantation: a spell or ceremony, spoken or sung, intended to produce some effect by magic

inscription: words carved on a stone surface, usually of a ceremonial nature

intermediate: in ancient Egyptian history, a period of time characterized by weak, disunified government between periods of strong, well-organized government

magic: the supposed ability to achieve, through special acts or objects, supernatural human control over the forces of nature and thus produce desired results

mastaba: the rectangular flat-topped structure built over early dynasty tombs; from an Arabic word meaning "bench"

mercenary: a soldier who serves, solely for pay, in the army of a country other than the soldier's

monotheism: the belief that there is only one god. Judaism, Christianity, and Islam are monotheistic religions; ancient Egyptian religion and Hinduism, for example, are polytheistic, believing in more than one god.

moral: having to do with principles of right and wrong in decisions and behavior

mythology: a particular group's collection of myths—stories, usually about deities or legendary heros, that attempt to explain the natural world or shed light on human existence

necropolis: a large cemetery

oasis: a well-watered, fertile place in a desert region

obelisk: a four-sided, slender stone shaft, tapering to a pointed top, usually covered with hieroglyphic inscriptions

pharaonic: pertaining to ancient Egypt from the start of the dynastic period until the Roman period

relief: pictures carved into the surface of stone

sanctuary: the most sacred part of a house of worship

substitution: the ancient Egyptian idea that small models or pictures of people and objects could substitute for the real thing in providing for a dead person's needs in the afterlife

tribute: money or goods paid to a more powerful government by groups or nations under the control or protection of that government

vizier: in ancient Egyptian government, the chief administrator under the king, something like a prime minister; an Arabic/Turkish word used by Egyptologists to describe this office

FOR FURTHER READING

Nonfiction

Harris, Geraldine. *Ancient Egypt: Cultural Atlas for Young People.* New York: Facts on File, 1990.

Harris, Geraldine. *Gods and Pharaohs from Egyptian Mythology.* New York: Peter Bedrick Books, 1992.

Mertz, Barbara. *Temples, Tombs and Hieroglyphs.* New York: Peter Bedrick Books, 1990; originally published, 1964.

Payne, Elizabeth. *The Pharaohs of Ancient Egypt.* New York: Knopf, 1981; originally published, 1964.

Perl, Lila. *Mummies, Tombs and Treasures.* New York: Clarion, 1987.

Stewart, Desmond. *The Pyramids and Sphinx.* New York: Newsweek Books, 1971.

Watterson, Barbara. *The Gods of Ancient Egypt.* New York: Facts on File, 1984.

Woods, Geraldine. *Science in Ancient Egypt.* New York: Franklin Watts, 1988.

Fiction

Bradshaw, Gillian. *The Dragon and the Thief.* New York: Greenwillow, 1991.

Carter, Dorothy Sharp. *His Majesty, Queen Hatshepsut.* New York: Lippincott, 1987.

Dexter, Catherine. *The Gilded Cat.* New York: Morrow Junior Books, 1992.

Harris, Rosemary. *The Bright and Morning Star.* New York: Macmillan, 1972.

McGraw, Eloise Jarvis. *The Golden Goblet.* New York: Coward McCann, 1961; Puffin, 1986.

McGraw, Eloise Jarvis. *Mara, Daughter of the Nile.* New York: Coward McCann, 1953; Puffin, 1985.

Morrison, Lucille. *The Lost Queen of Egypt.* New York: Lippincott, 1937.

Norton, Andre. *Shadow Hawk.* New York: Harcourt Brace, 1960.

Service, Pamela. *The Reluctant God.* New York: Atheneum, 1988.

Snyder, Zilpha Keatley. *The Egypt Game.* New York: Atheneum, 1967; Dell, 1986.

Stolz, Mary. *Cat in the Mirror.* New York: Harper & Row, 1975; New York: Dell, 1978.

BIBLIOGRAPHY

Breasted, James. *Development of Religion and Thought in Ancient Egypt.* New York: Charles Scribner's Sons, 1912, 1959.

David, A. Rosalie. *The Egyptian Kingdoms.* London: Elsevier, 1975.

Frankfort, H. *Ancient Egyptian Religion.* New York: Columbia University Press, 1948.

Frankfort, H. and H. A. Frankfort. *The Intellectual Adventure of Ancient Man.* Chicago: University of Chicago Press, 1946.

Hart, George. *Ancient Egypt.* Eyewitness Books. New York: Knopf, 1990.

James, T. G. H. *The Archaeology of Ancient Egypt.* Henry Z. Walck, 1972.

James, T. G. H. *Pharaoh's People: Scenes from Life in Imperial Egypt.* Chicago: University of Chicago Press, 1984.

Kaster, Joseph. *The Literature and Mythology of Ancient Egypt.* Penguin Press, 1968.

Rice, Michael. *Egypt's Making: The Origins of Ancient Egypt.* New York: Routledge, 1990.

Ruffle, John. *Heritage of the Pharaohs.* Oxford, England: Phaidon, 1977.

Spencer, A. J. *Early Egypt: The Rise of Civilisation in the Nile Valley.* London: British Museum, 1993.

Trigger, B. G., B. J. Kemp, D. O'Connor, and A. B. Lloyd. *Ancient Egypt: A Social History.* Cambridge, England: Cambridge University Press, 1983.

Wallis Budge, E. A. *Egyptian Magic.* London: Kegan Paul, 1899, 1988.

Wilson, John A. *The Burden of Egypt.* Chicago: University of Chicago Press, 1951.

INDEX

Page numbers for illustrations are in boldface

ABOUT THE AUTHOR

Growing up near Boston, Elsa Marston loved to visit the famous ancient Egyptian collection of the Museum of Fine Arts. She was inspired to write her first "novel"—about ancient Egypt—in the fourth grade. After earning a master's degree in international affairs at Harvard University, she went to the Middle East (Lebanon) and soon found her way to Egypt. Since then, she has lived in Cairo several times with her husband, Iliya Harik, a Middle Eastern specialist at Indiana University, and their three sons. Her recently published works for young people include *Lebanon: New Light in an Ancient Land*; the picture books *Cynthia and the Runaway Gazebo* and *A Griffin in the Garden*; and stories (one with an ancient Egyptian theme) in two collections for young adults, *Short Circuits* and *Join In: Multiethnic Short Stories*. Ms. Marston lives with her husband in Bloomington, Indiana.

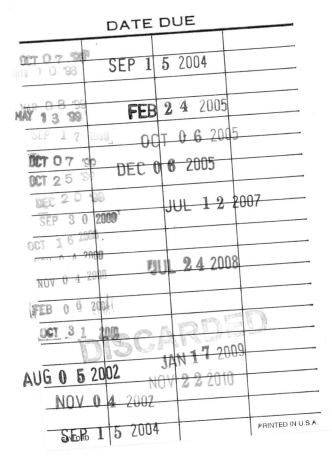